MY
SHADOW WORK
WORKBOOK

MY SHADOW WORK WORKBOOK

Text by Caitlin McAllister

An Hachette UK Company
www.hachette.co.uk

Vie Books, an imprint of Summersdale Publishers
Part of Octopus Publishing Group Limited
Carmelite House
50 Victoria Embankment
LONDON
EC4Y 0DZ
UK

www.summersdale.com

Printed and bound in China

ISBN: 978-1-83799-462-5

Substantial discounts on bulk quantities of Summersdale books are available to corporations, professional associations and other organizations. For details contact general enquiries: telephone: +44 (0) 1243 771107 or email: enquiries@summersdale.com.

MY SHADOW WORK WORKBOOK

*Guided Exercises to Help
You Find Self-Acceptance
and Inner Peace*

vie

CONTENTS

INTRODUCTION

As a child, you may have lived life as your unique, unfiltered self. Over the years your experiences and societal influences will have shaped your demeanour, edited your mindset and presented a version of yourself you have created in order to "fit in". These rejected parts of you did not disappear; they remain lingering in your subconscious and can pop up at times when you least expect them to.

Shadow Work can help you to bring repressed thoughts and experiences to the surface, and it's one of the most enlightening practices you can do for your mind. By getting to know the hidden parts of yourself, you will begin to excavate the real you, introduce yourself to the attributes and qualities you once unknowingly disowned and release any negative, unhelpful beliefs you hold.

The Shadow Work Workbook is designed to help you become your whole self, even if that means acknowledging parts that you don't initially like. By learning to integrate your shadow self into your life, you allow it to become part of your identity.

Shadow Work enables you to acknowledge the origins of your feelings, heal old wounds and gain clarity and catharsis from embracing your true self wholeheartedly. It's time to bring emotions to the surface, illuminate your subconscious and step into a new, empowered version of yourself.

Remember, dealing with hidden emotions and facing supressed personality traits might be difficult and confronting work, as it threatens your sense of identity. For this reason, you should progress through this workbook at your own pace and take regular breaks if you feel overwhelmed.

Part One:

What Is Shadow Work?

Shadow Work is an introspective psychological practice that can help you to expose subconscious thoughts, feelings and behaviours you consider to be your most undesirable traits. You may avoid revealing these parts of yourself to others or admitting they exist at all. Shadow Work can help you connect with these deeper parts of yourself to live a more holistic, authentic life.

How Can Shadow Work Help?

Shadow Work can be an incredibly powerful personal development tool that involves addressing inner demons and insecurities, healing from negative past experiences, getting to know your shadow self and integrating some of its helpful traits into your life without shame. Ultimately, the reward is a more realistic view of yourself, and greater satisfaction in life. With Shadow Work, you can unite suppressed elements of your personality with the version of yourself that currently exists in the world.

This book is designed to help you explore the different facets of your life and shed light on the parts of yourself that you have rejected over the years. With guided exercises and easy-to-follow advice, you can discover:

- **What Shadow Work is and why it can be a game-changer for happiness and fulfilment**

- **The essential techniques of the practice and how to apply them to your everyday life**

- **How to connect with buried experiences, face difficult emotions and challenge your inner critic**

- **How to love yourself unapologetically and live your life as your authentic self**

The History of Shadow Work

The idea of the "shadow" was made popular in the Western world in the early twentieth century by a Swiss psychiatrist and psychoanalyst called Carl Jung, who was a student of Sigmund Freud. Jung believed that our minds hold both conscious and unconscious beliefs about ourselves, and the unconscious parts live in the shadow part of our brain. This part represents any hidden aspect of ourselves that we may have repressed or denied over the years. Jung argued that our shadow self should not be viewed as a negative or shameful thing, but rather, as another important part of our personalities that should be incorporated with the parts we show to the world.

His theories informed the Shadow Work we know today, which unearths the elements of ourselves that we aren't aware of or don't want to acknowledge and teaches us how to bring some of these elements into our current lives.

Shadow Work has become an important tool for developing self-awareness. The concept integrates aspects of psychology, spirituality and self-discovery, so no matter your beliefs, you can find elements of Shadow Work that speak to you and use them to better understand and develop your identity.

Since its introduction, the practice of Shadow Work has evolved to become a fundamental element of personal development and many different types of therapy, including Jungian psychotherapy, Gestalt therapy and more. Shadow Work typically involves guided introspection with exercises like journalling and meditation which can help us uncover and integrate our shadow self into our daily lives.

Studies have found that emotional writing can decrease depressive symptoms, perceived stress and rumination in those with trauma. So working through the exercises in this book could bring you closer to understanding your anxieties, fears, negative thinking, anger issues and much more.

By exploring the hidden aspects of your own shadow throughout this book and engaging in the exercises to dig deeper into your psyche, you can achieve a greater sense of self-awareness and personal fulfilment that can begin to shape your life in a positive way.

The privilege of a lifetime is to become who you truly are.

CARL JUNG

What Is the Shadow?

The shadow is sometimes thought of as our "dark side" and may refer to less desirable traits and emotions such as anger, selfish tendencies, jealousy, greed and a desire for power or money. We may relegate specific elements of our personality if we feel that others may judge us for them, or they are universally considered "bad". Or we may equate those parts of ourselves with a negative experience or memory; there are several reasons our inherent traits can become part of our shadow, and often we don't even realize.

The shadow might consist of a number of elements of our psyche, hidden deep within us. These could be our thoughts, our feelings, mental images, attitudes, desires and motivations, judgements from others, judgements from ourselves and impulses.

The shadow is the engine that drives many of our behaviours. Everyone has one, whether or not they are aware of all of their own traits, or whether or not they choose to explore their shadow.

WHAT IF THE
HIDDEN PARTS
OF YOUR
PERSONALITY
TURNED OUT TO
BE THE KEY TO
YOUR HAPPINESS?

Light and shadow are opposite sides of the same coin. We can illuminate our paths or darken our way.

MAYA ANGELOU

The Process of Shadow Work

If you are interested in starting the potentially life-changing process of Shadow Work yourself then it is totally normal to be curious about what the practice actually looks like in action and what steps may be needed to bring you to a place of enlightenment. After all, Shadow Work can be a deeply emotional process and it's important to fully understand what you are getting yourself into.

At its most simple, Shadow Work is about:

1. **Getting to know your shadow = learning about the hidden and disowned parts of yourself, even if they make you feel uncomfortable**

2. **Integrating your shadow = bringing together the external and internal versions of yourself and making space to create the authentic you that you would like to become in future**

You can see a psychologist or mental health professional to work through their own preferred structure for Shadow Work. However, as you dip your toe in the water of Shadow Work, there are exercises you can do at home to further your understanding of yourself and start bringing these traits into your current life.

Stage 1:

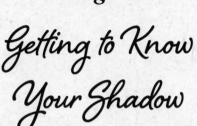

Getting to Know Your Shadow

The process of getting to know your shadow through Shadow Work is unique to you. This is because we all respond best to slightly different methods, in the same way that some of us learn best through pictures and videos while others retain more by writing things down. By leaning into your own learning style, you will discover which exercises and methods work for you.

Ways you might get to know your shadow:

- **Journalling to tap into the parts of you that have been shut off for a long time**

- **Talking with your inner child**

- **Acknowledging difficult past experiences**

- **Admitting to your biggest desires**

- **Looking closer at the most important relationships in your life**

- **Accepting responsibility for things that have gone wrong in the past (where applicable)**

… and more. Remember, some of the things that rise to the surface during Shadow Work could be things you had no idea existed, or they could be things that you already knew about yourself but didn't like or didn't want to acknowledge.

Stage 2:

Integrating Your Shadow

Once you have introduced yourself to your shadow and you start to understand what past experiences have led to you repressing certain parts of yourself, you can begin to integrate your shadow self with the version of you that exists on the outside.

This may include:

- **Exercising your self-compassion with daily acts of kindness to yourself**

- **Allowing yourself to react in a specific way in certain circumstances**

- **Being more attentive to your own needs and desires**

- **Being more intentional with the identity you are trying to create**

- **Challenging negative thought processes before they spiral**

- **Continuing with regular self-reflection work to maintain an open dialogue with your shadow**

… and more. Your shadow is made up of these disowned parts. Integrating it with your current self can help you to be more open to your natural instincts, react to life from a place of consciousness and be more authentically you.

PULL BACK THE
CURTAIN ON YOUR
INNER SELF AND
COMMIT TO FIERCELY
LOVING WHATEVER
YOU FIND

Identity versus Self-Identity

Many people go through life unaware that there is a distinction between their true identity and the identity they have constructed for themselves, otherwise known as self-identity. Our self-identity might not fully reflect our true selves and is often built using elements we have hand-picked from experiences and influences over the years, such as things we learned in university, traits we unknowingly copied from a parent, experiences we have had when searching for jobs, things our friends value highly or what the media influences us to think.

We often develop these traits as coping mechanisms in response to someone else's needs, but all of these things can be part of our identity, and we can acknowledge their important role in shaping who we are.

> *The beauty of Shadow Work is the ability to decide which of these self-identified traits we want to keep in our lives and which ones it's time to say goodbye to.*

Ultimately, our primarily positive self-identity can help to mask the underlying emotions we are guarding, desires we dare not admit to and beliefs we feel are protecting us. By acknowledging that our self-identity is not entirely truthful, we can start to peel back these layers and reveal our shadow self.

To be yourself in a world
that is constantly trying
to make you something
else is the greatest
accomplishment.

RALPH WALDO EMERSON

How Does the Shadow Form?

All shadows start somewhere, and as you read through this book you may start to connect the dots on where some parts of yours came from. Your shadow self may be formed from things like:

- **Early childhood experiences, particularly those involving trauma, neglect or other significant events***

- **Traumatic incidents that caused harm to you or others***

- **Experiences at school and in other educational environments where you were encouraged to adhere to rules**

- **Family dynamics teaching you how to interact with others, such as parental expectations or sibling rivalries**

- **Peer relationships within your social group, particularly in childhood**

- **Cultural and societal expectations of what is deemed acceptable or unacceptable behaviour**

- **Spiritual and religious teachings that certain traits are somehow sinful or shameful**

- **Major life changes that unearth hidden emotions and trigger deep desires**

Note: It is important to seek professional help from a mental health specialist if you are dealing with symptoms of past traumas.

When we experience these things how we choose to handle each situation outwardly influences the formation of our shadow self as we develop certain characteristics or desires as a coping mechanism and suppress complicated emotions. As a result, these feelings take up residence in our subconscious minds and become our shadow – the self that we want to hide so we can continue being accepted by others.

Our shadow continues to evolve throughout our lives thanks to each new experience.

THE SHADOW IN ACTION

An example of someone's shadow self staying hidden might be if an individual says "I don't care what people think of me" to give the outward impression that they are comfortable in their own skin. In reality, that person might find themselves regularly indulging in reckless impulse purchases of clothes they believe will make them look more desirable to a potential partner, or will make friends and colleagues take notice of them – this is the shadow emerging.

Despite self-identifying as someone who does not pander to others' expectations, their actions are telling a different story and giving a small insight into feelings, thoughts and emotions that could be hiding within their shadow.

Here's what this might look like:

- **Self-identity: "I don't care what people think of me"**
- **Shadow: Impulse spending on new clothes**
- **Possible negative past experience: Rejection from a peer**
- **Underlying fear: Being rejected again**

In this scenario, the individual is avoiding feelings of rejection by conveying to the external world that they don't care what others think of them. However, their shadow is breaking through by driving their urge to buy new clothes in an effort to impress people.

YOUR INNER CHILD IS TRYING TO TELL YOU SOMETHING. DON'T IGNORE THEM.

What Is the Inner Child?

The inner child is a psychological concept similar to the idea of the shadow self, as it refers to our innermost emotions and thoughts left behind from childhood. The belief is that we all have an inner child who still exists in our psyche as an adult, and for some this means they have certain needs and desires that have not yet been met.

The experiences we have during our formative years can be the most crucial; we may be influenced by adults around us, other children, reactions to our actions, perceptions of our successes and the like. The inner child essentially represents the unresolved emotional and psychological turmoil from our childhood, based on experiences we have had.

When most people picture their inner child, they usually see typical childlike traits like vulnerability, imagination and joy. When these characteristics are combined with positive childhood experiences, we may be met with a resilient and happy inner child. On the other hand, when these traits are combined with experiences like trauma or neglect, our inner child may have unresolved pain in adulthood.

This can show up in times of stress or can be triggered by external events. The responses we have learned during childhood can make us react in seemingly negative, immature or inappropriate ways.

By better understanding and nurturing the inner child, you can start to heal from past negative experiences and reconnect with a more authentic version of yourself.

Remember, allowing the inner child to have more say in your life does not mean you must regress to childish or childlike behaviours. It simply means you can acknowledge the unsettled feelings of your younger self, treat them with kindness and compassion, address them with the emotional regulation you have in adulthood and slowly start to integrate your inner child with your current life in a fulfilling way.

Where Does the Shadow Exist?

When we think of our shadow, we usually picture the dark shape cast by our bodies when standing next to a bright light. In fact, the "shadow", in the context of Shadow Work, is a metaphorical concept, so you won't find it in physical form. However, just because you can't see something doesn't mean it's not there.

You can experience the shadow showing up in various ways:

- **Parts of our personality that we don't like**
- **Aspects of other people's personalities that make us feel uncomfortable**
- **Our self-image**
- **Our insecurities**
- **Our fears**
- **Our darkest thoughts**
- **What we desire most in life**
- **Our response to external stimuli**
- **How we treat and communicate with other people**
- **Daily habits that we choose to engage in**
- **The things that trigger a negative reaction in us**
- **Traits or behaviours we judge in other people**
- **How we act when we feel attacked or judged ourselves**
- **"Big" feelings, like rage, despair or excitement**

While the shadow isn't something you can see or touch, there are lots of signs in our personalities and behaviours that give a strong indication of our underlying shadow self.

Seek to be whole,

not perfect.

OPRAH WINFREY

WHERE IS THE
REAL YOU HIDING?

Just as things like our triggers and insecurities can shine a light on what our shadow self really feels, there are some positive, neutral and negative parts of our personalities that can show through when we think about certain aspects of life.

For example, you might put 110 per cent effort into your career every day, but constantly feel guilty that you haven't visited your family in weeks. Or you might become obsessed with a new hobby every couple of months, abandoning the last one. Or you may suffer from extreme stress when Christmas comes around each year and wonder why it seems to be an annual feeling.

Learning about the real you means putting almost everything you do and think under the microscope – even the everyday reactions that you think have nothing to do with your shadow self could be the key to discovering what the real you needs. Once you figure this out, you can start to rebuild your identity.

On the next page, you will find a number of prompt questions. Take ten minutes for yourself today to sit and think about the answers to a few of these.

What do people tell you that you are great at? When they tell you this, do you enjoy the compliment, or do you feel shy?

What hobbies or interests could you do for hours on end without interruption?

What stresses you out the most each day, week, month or year?

Does anyone ever tell you that you "go overboard" on certain things? If so, why do you think this is?

Do you ever find yourself doing things you don't want to do for other people? If so, why?

Is there anything you absolutely hate? If so, why do you think you have such a strong reaction to it?

Is there anything you would love to do in your life that you aren't already doing? If so, why haven't you done it yet?

YOUR SHADOW IS HIDING YOUR AUTHENTIC, REAL, BRILLIANT SELF

The Importance of Self-Awareness

Self-awareness means having a conscious recognition of your own thoughts, behaviours and emotions. It is an important element of Shadow Work as it can create a foundation for meaningful transformation by allowing you more clarity on how you come across in the world, how your feelings affect your actions and what you really want in life.

In the context of Shadow Work, self-awareness can mean identifying repressed feelings that hide in your shadow. So it is extremely important to develop your sense of self-awareness to make Shadow Work successful.

Without self-awareness, your personal growth journey would be more difficult as you would be unable to tell where you started from, where you are now and when you have become the person you want to be. Ultimately, self-awareness fosters authenticity and a stronger connection with the self – it is like an internal compass that can show you the direction to go in next.

*To know yourself,
you must sacrifice
the illusion that
you already do.*

VIRONIKA TUGALEVA

SELF-AWARENESS IS
THE ONLY PATH TO
PERSONAL GROWTH.
TAKE STOCK,
TAKE STEPS.

Insight Page

Throughout this book you will find several Insight Pages that you can use to write down anything you learn about yourself while on your Shadow Work journey. Record any lightbulb moments in these pages and look back on them later. You can do this in the space below.

You could write down any difficult emotions that led you to pick up this book, or explore what your personal goals of Shadow Work might be. This space is yours to use as you wish.

....

....

....

....

....

....

....

....

....

....

....

....

....

The authentic self is
the soul made visible.

SARAH BAN BREATHNACH

The Dangers of *Ignoring Your Shadow*

You cannot ignore your shadow. You can try to, but there are a number of problems that tend to rise to the surface when you repress thoughts and feelings. Ignoring the shadow can cause it to force its way into the light when you least expect or want it to, with less desirable emotions and reactions bubbling to the surface. Ignoring the shadow can lead to many unpleasant feelings and responses:

Unhelpful thoughts and behaviours

Repetitive patterns

Poor self-esteem

Feeling disconnected or fragmented

Self-sabotage

Stress

Anxiety

Unresolved trauma

Depression

Misguided life choices

Intense emotional outbursts

Missed opportunities

Blockages
when trying to
form connections
with others

Relationship
challenges

Never feeling
like the real "you"

Projecting emotions
onto others

Not progressing
with personal growth

Destructive
habits*

Being unable
to reach your full
potential in life

Physical symptoms
such as pain or discomfort

Addictive behaviours, such
as alcohol abuse or gambling*

Note: *If you are engaging in destructive or addictive behaviours, you should reach out to a professional or relevant service as early as possible so they can provide you with useful resources and tools and break the cycle before it progresses further.*

When someone attempts to ignore their shadow for too long, eventually the effects of any underlying emotions will make themselves known, so being proactive with Shadow Work is the best way to work through and heal from anything that may be lingering in the subconscious.

Doing the Work

Shadow Work can be difficult at times, and it should be committed to as a journey in its entirety in order to achieve genuinely profound personal growth. This means that a combination of courage and consistency is needed.

When our negative shadow starts to turn our life upside down during Shadow Work, it is important to fully finish what we started by working through any emotions related to the negative shadow and to take the time to properly introduce them into our everyday lives. Always commit to finishing Shadow Work practices so you can resolve feelings and leave nothing unsettled.

There may be missed opportunities to fully know yourself and become the person you need to be if you were to set off on a transformative journey only to turn back halfway. Commit to the work and protect your mindset throughout.

Protect Yourself

It is easy to become overwhelmed during the process of Shadow Work, as you may be dissecting old memories, thinking about difficult relationships in your life and facing parts of yourself that are uncomfortable to acknowledge.

Engaging in Shadow Work requires a lot of self-care and compassion in order to protect your mental health throughout the entire process. This is where self-awareness can be incredibly helpful. With healthy self-awareness, you can predict when you will need to take a step back, use kinder language, create boundaries and so on.

A few ways you can protect your mindset during Shadow Work:

Establish
a routine

Add mindful practices to
your day, like meditation
and journalling

Take breaks
when needed

Sit with
any intense
emotions

Give yourself time to
heal between Shadow
Work exercises

Seek therapy
if you think it
could help

Build a support
network

Keep in mind that you should definitely seek professional guidance from a licensed therapist if you are working through unresolved trauma.

COMMIT TO YOUR MENTAL HEALTH JOURNEY...

... FACE SHADOWS,
EMBRACE
DISCOVERY, KEEP
BLOOMING AND
NEVER BE AFRAID
TO ASK FOR HELP

The Life Benefits
of Shadow Work

Shadow Work is uncomfortable, confronting, and can shake up some very difficult emotions, so... why do it?

Ultimately, while Shadow Work can feel like a negative thing at the time, it has so many transformative, empowering benefits that make it a worthwhile pursuit. Also, it can leave you with positive ripple effects throughout every aspect of your life.

There are many benefits to Shadow Work:

A feeling of profound personal growth

Stronger relationships with others

Better emotional resilience

Clearer self-awareness

Greater authenticity

Insight into thought patterns

Less reactive to emotional triggers

More intentional decision-making

A deeper understanding of motivations and desires

Resolved negative symptoms from past traumas

Better able to
express yourself

Lower levels of stress,
anxiety or depression

Reduced
self-sabotaging
behaviours

Feeling aligned
with your true values

Go after what
you really desire

Explore
untapped
talents

Feel more
fulfilled in life

Have a better
understanding of
past experiences

Emotionally heal
from past traumas

Increased capacity and
ability to contribute to
your larger community

Although Shadow Work can be uncomfortable to engage in while doing it, it is clear that without it we could all be trapped in many more years of not fully understanding ourselves, not expressing our true emotions and not fulfilling our full potential in life.

If something is particularly challenging during your Shadow Work journey, you should lean into this in your own time. It is so important to protect your mental health and take breaks when needed, but when you feel ready to tackle the most difficult parts of Shadow Work, try to reach a place where you feel that particular shadow is resolved.

Nobody can hurt me without my permission.

MAHATMA GANDHI

IF YOU REDEFINE
YOUR NARRATIVE,
YOUR SHADOWS
CAN BECOME
YOUR BIGGEST
SUPERPOWERS

Knowing yourself
is the beginning
of all wisdom.

ARISTOTLE

Part Two:

Laying the Foundations

*Before you embark on your own Shadow Work journey,
there are some foundational steps that can help you to begin
looking inward. By acquiring some key skills to prepare,
you can learn to be more honest with yourself, have an
open mind, be kind and compassionate with your emotions
and recognize your own reactions, and much more.*

The Story of You

Have you ever thought about what you might say if you were on a talk show telling the presenter your life story? From your childhood influences and what you wanted to be when you grew up, to what your hobbies and interests are now, to your biggest life dreams and goals, there is a LOT to say when it comes to your life story – no matter what age you are or background you come from.

Before you begin your Shadow Work journey, it can help to take stock of where you are now and everything that has led you to this point. As you continue through Shadow Work, your perception of these things might change, but knowing how you currently feel about your life is a great place to start.

You could begin by imagining you are writing a memoir. What would each chapter be titled? What significant moments would be included? What memories are worth mentioning? What were you most passionate about as a child versus what are you most passionate about now? What things have you always found to be challenging in school or work? What would you feel most vulnerable about revealing in a memoir? What are your biggest strengths?

IT'S TIME TO
REWRITE YOUR
STORY AND BECOME
THE PERSON YOU
WERE ALWAYS
MEANT TO BE

Insight Page

Take some time in a quiet space by yourself and make notes about your life story so far, either here on this Insight Page or in your own notebook. Perhaps start by writing a contents page, noting down the chapter titles for significant stages of your life's journey, starting from childhood to where you are now.

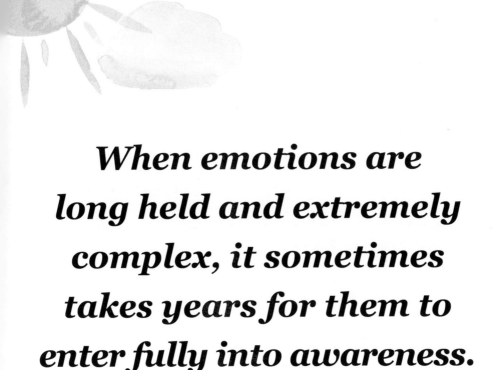

When emotions are long held and extremely complex, it sometimes takes years for them to enter fully into awareness.

SHARON SALZBERG

Understanding Emotions

Some experts say that the average person is thought to have more than 400 emotional experiences every day. Perhaps this can be hard to understand since many of us can't even name 400 emotions. Other studies suggest that people experience at least one emotion 90 per cent of the time. This may feel more in line with your own daily emotional journey.

By understanding and being able to acknowledge more of our daily emotions, we can develop our self-awareness, be more focused during mindfulness and learn not to simply observe our emotions without judging them. Mastering this can help with Shadow Work as it makes it much easier to analyze how you are feeling, why you might be feeling a certain way and what could make you feel better.

You won't be able to engage in Shadow Work without facing complicated emotions, so the sooner you start to pay attention to how you are feeling, the sooner you can start to experience breakthroughs.

Tap into your emotions more:

- **Pay attention to how your body feels and where emotions might be manifesting: Do you feel any tension? Have you changed your posture? Is there any pain or discomfort?**

- **Actively reflect by setting aside time alone without distractions to ponder the origins of some of your emotions.**

- **Get used to asking "why?" for every emotion that you feel. For example, if you feel uncomfortable in a certain social situation, examine this feeling.**

- **Practise emotional integration by avoiding labelling an emotion as either "good" or "bad". Try to consider all emotions as neutral and know that each one has its place on the full emotional spectrum and can be useful in certain situations.**

If you check in with your emotions more often, this process may gradually cement itself in your mind so that when something negative happens, you may be better able to acknowledge your negative emotions and move past them faster.

The Emotions Wheel

The Wheel of Emotions – designed by psychologist Dr Robert Plutchik – can help you to start acknowledging more of your emotions in everyday life. These are grouped together using the eight primary emotions that form the foundation of all other emotions. The eight emotions are joy and sadness, acceptance and disgust, fear and anger, and surprise and anticipation.

Use the Emotions Wheel below to pinpoint at least three emotions you feel in the next 24 hours. Remember, you might only notice experiencing one emotion and that's OK, but try to be open-minded and consider if any other emotions were present.

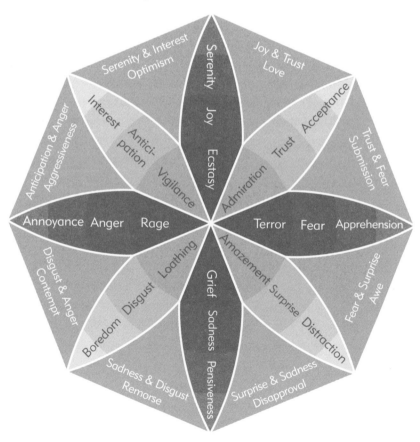

Expressing Emotions

Have you ever thought about how you express your emotions? Do you cry often? Get over-excited? Become angry easily? Take deep breaths when something doesn't go to plan? There is no "wrong" way to communicate your emotions, and you should never feel bad for being "too emotional" or "not emotional enough". Everyone has a different way of naturally showing emotions and learning to express yours in an authentic way can help you on your Shadow Work journey.

Start by being honest with yourself and acknowledging the emotions that come up most in your life, whether you feel these are positive or negative. Seek healthy communication with others and choose the best time and place to share anything that's on your mind. Focus on taking ownership of your feelings without blaming anyone else and allow others around you to express their emotions, too.

Remember, there are more ways to express emotions than just smiling or crying. Verbal communication might be your main way of expressing yourself, or you might choose to write things down, produce some sort of artwork or do something physical in order to express how you really feel. By understanding the many ways to express emotions, you can start to notice these in your own life and in others around you.

One does not become
enlightened by imagining
figures of light, but by making
the darkness conscious.

CARL JUNG

YOUR REACTIONS
CAN BE A WINDOW TO
YOUR REAL FEELINGS.
LET THE LIGHT
SHINE THROUGH.

Reactions =
Hidden Emotions

One of the best ways to experience the shadow taking over is to observe your reactions to certain situations and people. Often the way we react to things (particularly negative situations) can shed light on the parts of ourselves that we don't like.

We all have emotions beneath the surface, and when we are put in a particular situation our immediate response can act as a window into how we really feel about something underneath our camouflage.

An example of this might be someone reacting with a sudden burst of anger when in fact what they are really feeling is fear. Such defensive reactions are triggered by something underlying, and this might be an instance of being insecure in the past or reliving a previous trauma. Whatever the reason, it is always worth exploring anything that tends to cause an extreme reaction for you, as a little bit of introspection could alert you to an underlying emotion you weren't aware you were feeling.

When a strong reaction occurs, you might want to excuse yourself from the situation for a minute (if you can) and ask yourself questions like: "What am I really feeling in this situation?", "Why am I so triggered by this?" or "What emotions am I avoiding here?"

This may take some vulnerability, honesty and self-awareness, but the reward will be so worth it and could help you start to avoid feeling such a strong negative reaction in similar situations in future.

By better understanding the connection between our reactions and what lies beneath them, we can have more control and autonomy over our responses and express our emotions in a healthier way.

Here are some more examples of what initial reactions could mean:

- **A sudden burst of anger at an unexpected turn of events could be masking insecurity felt after a loss of control over a past situation**

- **Initial guardedness could be a defence mechanism against possible rejection based on a past experience**

- **An intense urge to avoid a situation could be the mind's way of protecting against hurt from an old betrayal**

- **Making light of a serious situation could be a cover for underlying emotions of discomfort**

- **A knee-jerk decision to ignore something or pretend it's not happening could be due to past shame that hasn't been dealt with**

How to Analyze Your Reactions

When our initial reactions could be masking underlying emotions we aren't yet aware of, how do we *become* aware of them? Analyzing your responses takes a certain amount of self-awareness and a desire to become more in tune with your true feelings.

You should always observe your reactions without judgement by acknowledging that everyone reacts in ways they don't want to sometimes, and your initial response probably came from a place of protection based on past experiences.

It can help to ask questions straight after a reaction like:

- **What emotions broke through the surface?**
- **Was my reaction disproportionate to the situation?**
- **Where in my body do I feel tension?**
- **Could this be a trigger from a past experience? If so, which one?**
- **Now that I am approaching the situation from a calmer place, do I still feel the same? If not, what has changed?**

If you find it difficult to analyze your responses, a Reaction Journal could be helpful. This could be something you write in your phone so you have access to it on the go. It's where you could write down the triggering event, your emotional response, any conscious thoughts you had, anything you believe could be underlying and anything else relevant. Over time, you might notice patterns in your thoughts and see which areas of Shadow Work could be useful for you to work on further.

The person you call an enemy is an exaggerated aspect of your own shadow self.

DEEPAK CHOPRA

~~CONTROLLING~~
ACCEPTING YOUR REACTION

When it becomes clear that an initial reaction is not a clear representation of how you want to feel or behave, the worst thing you can do is judge yourself for it. We all flare up unexpectedly sometimes, and we all say and do things in the heat of an intense moment that we later reflect on and wish we could replay.

The difference between being emotionally mature and immature is in how you view your intense reaction to an event. When you notice an intense reaction you don't like in yourself, you can choose to observe it, analyze it and move on from it with a little more knowledge about your psyche than you did before. That is emotional maturity. That is self-awareness in action.

When we judge our reactions, we only add to our shame and discomfort, because we are essentially further suppressing our shadow self. One important part of Shadow Work is acknowledging your reactions as something very normal and human and integrating this element of your shadow into your current self. In time this will give you more autonomy over the external reactions you have.

The key to mastering acceptance of your initial reactions is to not attempt to control them (so long as they aren't putting yourself or anyone in danger), as this can lead to heightened stress and internal conflict that makes you feel worse and further distances you from your true emotions. Embracing your reactions and treating yourself with self-compassion creates a foundation for positive mental health.

That said, accepting your reaction does not mean you endorse it, and you should still aim for a healthier reaction in future that does not risk hurting anyone else around you. Consider whether you need to apologize for a knee-jerk response (it's OK if you do) and always make an effort to do this. This might even be a gateway to an honest conversation with a loved one about how certain triggers make you feel and how they can support you in better managing your reactions.

So often our attempts to control reactions stem from societal or self-imposed expectations, and being honest with someone else about why you feel a strong need to fit this mould can provide further insight into your shadow.

Emotional Intelligence and How to Develop It

Much of analyzing your emotions and being self-aware comes down to having something called emotional intelligence.

Emotional intelligence is an ability to recognize and manage your own emotions, while also having empathy and understanding of the emotions of others around you. Personal growth and Shadow Work require emotional intelligence as they need a certain amount of emotional analysis to get to the bottom of what lies beneath what others may see on the surface. Having healthy emotional intelligence can mean:

- **Recognizing initial reactions versus underlying feelings**
- **Reflecting on your emotions and response patterns regularly**
- **Managing impulses in stressful situations**
- **Practising empathy and taking the time to listen to/ understand others' perspectives**
- **Improving your ability to communicate**
- **Enhancing your social skills**
- **Improving collaboration and conflict resolution**
- **Fostering better relationships through honesty**

When we learn to embrace emotional intelligence as a continuous learning journey, we can start to value the role emotions play in personal growth.

EVERY EXPERIENCE YOU HAVE GROWS YOUR EMOTIONAL INTELLIGENCE

How you react emotionally is a choice in any situation.

JUDITH ORLOFF

Understanding What Energizes and Drains You

Our emotions and reactions are very often driven by the things around us that either energize us or drain us. Having awareness of what these things might be for us is one of the best ways to maintain emotional well-being, optimize our interactions with others and gain insight into our shadow self.

Think about the activities, environments and relationships you have in your life; which of these tend to deplete your energy? When you know what these things are, you can start to establish boundaries and prioritize self-care and compassion around these things to avoid burnout.

Similarly, which of these tend to boost your energy? When it is clear which social interactions, creative pursuits and environments do this for you, you can focus your time on these and bring more joy and fulfilment into your life.

Knowing your energy boosters versus your energy drainers can empower you to make choices each day that contribute positively to your mental health.

Embracing Failure

For many of us, hidden deep in our shadow are the failures we have experienced over the years. No matter what age you are, you will have at least one memory of "failing" and how that made you feel.

It's time to reframe the idea of failure, because ultimately failures are just lessons, and there is so much we can learn from them. The end goal of this mindset shift is to reach a place where, no matter what setbacks occur, you will start to see them less as insurmountable obstacles and more as opportunities for learning and improvement.

1. **Analyze the situation objectively – is there anything you can do to control it?**

2. **Find the lesson in the experience – what could you learn from this?**

3. **Consider what went wrong – what could you do better next time?**

4. **Find the positive in the situation – what is one positive thing you could say here?**

5. **Come up with a mantra – something like "Failure is not a reflection of my worth, it is simply a stepping stone towards my goal."**

A lack of self-love can cause us to be especially sensitive to our perceived failures and ignorant of our successes in life. It is important to shift your perspective and see mistakes less as indicators of inadequacy, and more as nuggets of feedback.

EMBRACE FAILURE
WITH BOTH HANDS.
NO ONE HAS EVER
DONE ANYTHING
WORTHWHILE
WITHOUT A
LITTLE FAILURE.

Insight Page

You could use this page or your own notebook to write down the three biggest "failures" you can remember from your life so far, and reframe them. You may find it helpful to consider how you would speak to your inner child if they made any of these mistakes, and address your leftover childhood emotions and feelings.

If you own this story you get to write the ending.

BRENÉ BROWN

Taking Responsibility

Shadow Work often delves into some tricky areas of our minds. When other people are involved in our negative experiences and injustices, it can be difficult to move past blame when we may have been deeply hurt and affected by someone else's actions. Taking responsibility for actions is something we all learn early on in life, but this lesson doesn't always stick.

This is not about ignoring the damaging actions and the hurt that others have caused us in the past, as accountability is important. However, one of the most effective ways to move past a difficult memory involving the blaming of others is to reframe the experience and accept responsibility for the parts of the situation *you* were in control of. An example of this might be:

- **Situation: My colleague was offered a promotion instead of me, but we started in the company at the same time**

- **Blame: I am angry at my manager for giving my colleague the promotion**

- **Taking responsibility: I am frustrated with myself for not putting in as much effort into my job as my colleague has over the past year**

- **Acceptance: I didn't get the promotion because I chose to prioritize my self-care this year instead of working extra hours**

Taking responsibility for everything that happens in your life can be a very powerful practice. We cannot change the past actions of others, and with the onus on them there is no real way to move past a perceived injustice. However, by taking the responsibility back into your own hands, you can acknowledge the control you had over a situation, reframe it as a lesson learned, and reclaim some of your own power.

This practice is much more difficult to apply to major life tragedies and betrayals, but not impossible. You may be completely against taking any sort of responsibility for something that has hurt you a lot, but remember you do not need to tell anyone or acknowledge this in a public way – as long as you can reflect on it yourself, you can gain the mental health benefits of closure. For example:

- **Situation: My partner was unfaithful**
- **Blame: I am angry at my partner for betraying my trust and ruining our relationship**
- **Taking responsibility: I am frustrated with myself for not seeing the signs earlier that we are not meant to be together**
- **Acceptance: I chose to love and trust someone with an open heart, and I would rather be a loving, trusting person than someone who is closed off to these emotions**

Taking personal responsibility, even when external circumstances influence your life, means accepting that ultimately your own responses, choices and actions are the things that shape your experience. With this mindset, you can become more proactive about your destiny rather than being a passive recipient of life's circumstances, and you can make more intentional choices about your goals by taking decisive action for your future.

IF YOU ARE
HOLDING ON TO
BLAME, IT'S TIME
TO RELEASE IT AND
FEEL LIGHTER

Insight Page

How are you feeling about your Shadow Work journey so far? Write down any lightbulb moments you have had, anything you might have learned about your shadows, and anything you want to look back on and remember later.

IT'S TIME TO ACCEPT THE PARTS OF YOURSELF THAT YOU DISOWNED A LONG TIME AGO...

... AND INVITE THEM INTO YOUR LIFE AGAIN

Life is 10 per cent what happens to you and 90 per cent how you react to it.

CHARLES R. SWINDOLL

All About the Ego

We cannot talk about Shadow Work without acknowledging the ego. The ego is the psychological construct that supports our sense of self-esteem and self-importance in relation to the reality around us. The concept has roots in Freudian theory, which suggested that the ego exists to balance the conflicting demands of our subconscious and the expectations we have on ourselves from external sources. We need the ego in order to navigate daily life with confidence and individuality, but it can also show up to the party with some of our most undesirable traits, such as self-centredness, stubbornness and pride.

The ego is discussed regularly in Shadow Work as it offers a window to some of our internal feelings, but ultimately a healthy, balanced ego is the goal. This means fostering self-awareness so you can recognize its influence in daily life and avoid letting it dictate all decisions, become arrogant or cloud your judgement.

Ego versus Shadow

In Shadow Work, the ego can be problematic as it can put up a wall when we are trying to reach a place of vulnerability and honesty. To differentiate the ego from the shadow:

- **Ego =** A mostly conscious part of our mind that balances our instinctual desires and societal expectations to help us navigate everyday life with a sense of self-awareness. Although some people may appear unaware of their own ego, it is considered a conscious part of our mind.

- **Shadow =** A subconscious, repressed aspect of our mind that harbours emotions, traits and desires we might think to be unacceptable or undesirable to others. The shadow is considered a subconscious part of our mind.

The ego is part of the reason we suppress many of our emotions to the shadow realms as its job is to make us look good in front of other people and society. For this reason, these two conflicting elements of our psychology continue to battle against each other in day-to-day life, but learning to manage this and create a healthy balance can help you start to feel more at peace with your shadow self and your ego.

It is easy to demonize the ego as the thing stopping your shadow self from emerging, but remember there are a number of ways the ego can have a positive influence on your life, including:

- **Increasing your self-confidence to put yourself forward in social situations**

- **Increasing your self-assurance, which could help you to tackle challenges and pursue goals with determination**

- **Strengthening your emotional resilience when under stress**

- **Motivating you to achieve things, reach success and strive for self-improvement**

- **Helping you to understand and adapt to the world around you, including the people you encounter**

- **Developing resilience to bounce back from any setbacks or perceived failures**

- **Offering a sense of independence so you feel comfortable making decisions**

- **Allowing you to be assertive in situations where you must express your opinion or boundaries**

We're afraid that if we show these ugly, unpalatable parts of ourselves, it will be too much for others.

EVANNA LYNCH

Insight Page

Can you think of ways when your ego has had a positive effect on your life and relationships? Write down any instances you can think of when your ego has been beneficial. For example, giving you confidence to overcome a setback or helping you to achieve something you might initially have been fearful of trying.

....
....
....
....
....
....
....
....
....
....
....
....
....
....
....
....
....
....

IF YOU ARE EMBARRASSED, IT'S ONLY BECAUSE YOU CARE DEEPLY ABOUT SOMETHING THAT YOU ARE TRYING TO PROTECT

Part Three:

Illuminate Your Shadows

It's time to put everything you have learned so far into practice with some helpful guided exercises designed to help you illuminate your shadow self. By working through these pages, you can figure out why your shadows exist in the first place, acknowledge and accept the reasons, and begin to integrate them into your life in a positive way.

Throw a Shadow Dinner Party

Shadow Work doesn't have to be intensely emotional – you can make it fun and experiment with different ways of exploring your shadow self.

Imagine you are throwing a dinner party and writing an invite list of all the different facets of your shadow you would like to attend. Give each one a name and imagine what they might say. For example, Embarrassed Emily might recount the time she tripped during the school show, or Blamer Bill might complain about how others have wronged him. By giving them all a seat at the table, you allow them to release emotions without judgement and move on.

- ....
  ....
- ....
  ....
- ....
  ....
- ....
  ....
- ....
  ....

HOLD SPACE FOR
YOUR SHADOW

Be yourself...

... not your idea of what you think somebody else's idea of yourself should be.

HENRY DAVID THOREAU

SPEAK TO YOUR SHADOW

Part of Shadow Work is learning how to communicate with the parts of yourself that you have silenced for a long time. While many people will shy away from the idea of speaking out loud to their shadow, there are ways you can do this without feeling awkward or having to talk to yourself. Why not try:

Meditation – Sit with your eyes closed somewhere you feel comfortable, take deep breaths and consider what your shadow might need from you. Perhaps you could start by answering the question: What is stopping me from being vulnerable by communicating with my shadow self?

Journalling – Find a blank page (or use one of the Insight Pages) and write down what you think your shadow self is trying to tell you. Answer the question: What has been playing on your mind recently?

Visualization – Sit quietly with a mirror in front of you and imagine your inner child sitting opposite you. Remember, your inner child represents your innermost emotions and thoughts left over from your childhood. Try to answer thequestion: What does my inner child need me to acknowledge in order to move on?

DON'T BE
AFRAID TO TALK
TO YOURSELF,
OR TO LISTEN
WHEN YOUR SELF
TALKS BACK

It is only through shadows that one comes to know the light.

ST CATHERINE OF SIENA

TAKE A MINUTE TO YOURSELF EACH DAY TO GET TO KNOW "YOU" AGAIN

Accept Your Shadow

Have you ever had a friend compliment you on something you always assumed was a negative trait? Acceptance from others makes us feel good, but we often forget it's possible to give *ourselves* this gift, too.

Use these prompts to acknowledge one of your shadow parts, and show it some compassion:

- **Something I've never liked about myself is:**

  ....

  ....

- **This part of me causes me discomfort because:**

  ....

  ....

- **One good thing about this part of me is:**

  ....

  ....

- **I want to embrace this part of me because:**

  ....

  ....

- **I can turn this part of me into a positive trait by:**

  ....

  ....

Lessons in Self-Love

Go back to your dinner party invite list and write out your different shadow parts here. For every shadow you feel sadness, anger, shame or resentment for add a message of self-love. In *every* situation you will be able to dig deep and find at least one positive thing if you really try.

SHADOW	SELF-LOVE

GIVE YOUR INNER
CHILD TIME EACH
DAY – EVEN JUST
A TINY MOMENT
– TO GET SILLY

Reaction Analysis

Our shadow self can emerge when we least expect it. It could be triggered by an external circumstance or a person, leading us to project our own insecurities onto others. Think back to a time when something evoked a strong emotional reaction in you, such as a setback to a plan, a challenge you needed to overcome, criticism from a peer or even something positive like praise from a friend. Put it under the microscope by answering the following questions:

1. Name a situation that caused you to have strong feelings. (Example: My friends went out for dinner without inviting me.)

....

....

....

2. What was your initial reaction? (Example: I wanted to call them to ask why I had been excluded.) What feelings came up at that moment? (Example: I was angry, upset and felt left out.)

....

....

....

3. Could this be connected to any qualities you don't like about yourself? (Example: Maybe I am disappointed in myself because I'm always cancelling on them due to social anxiety.)

....

....

....

4. Could this be connected to a past incident that caused you stress? (Example: I was once left out of a school play because I was too scared to audition for it.)

....

....

....

5. How could you explore this shadow further in future? (Example: I could spend more time listening to my inner child to unpack this memory of the school play, and ask my shadow self why I tend to cancel plans.)

....

....

....

Get Creative

Discovering your shadow can be a lot of fun as you learn more and more interesting things about yourself. Although there can be some difficult emotions to work through, don't forget to enjoy the process too! There are many types of creative therapy – such as art therapy – that can help people who struggle to verbalize their feelings.

Use the space below to get creative in any way you choose, perhaps draw a picture of your shadow self.

You can't use up
creativity. The more you
use, the more you have.

MAYA ANGELOU

OUR HABITS
AND BELIEFS ARE
FORMED OVER
MANY YEARS,
BUT THEY CAN
BE UNFORMED
AT ANY POINT.

DECONSTRUCT
WHAT YOU THINK
YOU KNOW AND
BE OPEN TO A
NEW VERSION
OF YOURSELF.

Exploring the Past

If you have complicated emotions to work through, it can help to revisit past experiences that may have impacted your current life. Use these journal prompts to analyze any experiences that may have led to certain habits, beliefs or behaviours today.

- **If you could revisit one moment from your life, what would it be?**

- **What do you consider to be one of the worst things that has ever happened to you, and what shadow traits have formed as a result?**

- **List the three most important relationships in your life. How might they have impacted on your shadow self, positively or negatively?**

Remember*: Shadow Work is a helpful tool, but it should not be used as a substitute for professional therapy if you have experienced traumas such as violence or neglect.*

Resistance by definition is self-sabotage.

STEVEN PRESSFIELD

HABIT ORIGINS

Whether good or bad, we all have habits that have formed over years of reinforcement. Identifying where these habits might have come from, such as shutting down as a way to protect your emotions, can help you to better understand why you do the things you do. It can also help you see ways to change them if you would like to.

Write out some of the habits you have noticed about yourself and identify where you think each habit originated.

Habit 1:
....

Origin of habit 1:
....

....

Habit 2:
....

Origin of habit 2:
....

....

Habit 3:
....

Origin of habit 3:
....

....

Habit 4:
....

Origin of habit 4:
....

....

Habit 5:
....

Origin of habit 5:
....

....

BELIEF ORIGINS

Similar to our habits, our beliefs will have been shaped over years of experiences, and knowing their origins is often the first step to reframing them.

Write out some of the beliefs you hold strongly and identify what might have influenced each one.

Belief 1:
....
Influence on belief 1:
....

....

Belief 2:
....
Influence on belief 2:
....

....

Belief 3:
....
Influence on belief 3:
....

....

Belief 4:
....
Influence on belief 4:
....

....

Belief 5:
....
Influence on belief 5:
....

....

DON'T LET
SELF-SABOTAGE
GET IN THE WAY
OF THE AMAZING
IDEAS YOU HAVE
TO SHARE, AND
THE AMAZING
PERSON YOU ARE
AT YOUR CORE

Your self-worth is determined by you. You don't have to depend on someone telling you who you are.

BEYONCÉ

No More Self-Sabotage

If Shadow Work is bringing you closer to the life you want to lead, you cannot let self-sabotage get in the way by restricting your ability to achieve your goals. Read between the lines of such behaviours to allow your shadows to surface. If you know you have a tendency to self-sabotage, explore why this might be.

I think I self-sabotage when I'm faced with ....
....

When this happens, I can't seem to ....
....

and it leads to me feeling ....
....

I am committed to stopping the self-sabotage cycle, and I will do this by ....
....

I know accountability is helpful for self-sabotaging traits, so when I feel an urge to ....
....

I will speak to .... for advice and encouragement.

Challenging the Good and Celebrating the Bad

Not all of a person's positive traits should be considered "good", just as not all negative traits should be considered "bad". Instead of letting our ego take over with the good traits and repressing the bad ones, we can learn to challenge what we think is inherently good about us and celebrate what we have always considered to be bad.

Use the boxes below to write out what you want to challenge, and what you want to celebrate:

I WILL CHALLENGE...

I WILL CELEBRATE...

DREAM ANALYSIS

During REM sleep, our minds tend to sort through subconscious thoughts and feelings, and assign them to our mental filing cabinets. This has been proven by neuroscience, with the active parts of our brain helping to generate images in the mind while we sleep.

These images can come from memories, desires, fears and a number of other subconscious thoughts, so interpreting dreams can give insight into our shadow self. If you have regular dreams, it can help to write down anything you remember so you can start to look for patterns and points of interest.

Remember, sometimes dreams are only memorable in the first few minutes after sleep, so keep this book or your own notebook near your bed so you can record anything notable as soon as you wake.

Use the following page to capture the next significant dream you have, or to write notes about what usually happens in a recurring dream, if you have one.

DREAM NOTES

I THINK THIS DREAM MEANS...

Who Do You Admire?

Recognizing negative traits in others can shine a light on the things we need to work on ourselves, but what about the traits we admire in others? Having admiration for someone – whether it's someone we love or someone notable we take inspiration from – can give us insight into the qualities we would like to develop in ourselves.

Think about the people you really respect and list the things you like most about them. Then, consider how you could bring their best traits into your own life.

I admire...

I want to emulate this by...

Resilience

One of the most important aspects of Shadow Work to master is the art of resilience. When you are constantly analysing the darkest parts of yourself, it can be difficult to keep showing up and doing the work, so resilience is key.

Affirmations are words of wisdom you can call upon whenever you need a mental boost. Use the space below to write three affirmations you can come back to any time you need to get back on the horse. For example, "Shadow Work is difficult, but I'm already making progress and becoming a better 'me'."

1.

....

....

....

2.

....

....

....

3.

....

....

....

FLOWERS DON'T LET THE STONES IN THEIR WAY STOP THEM FROM GROWING AS TALL AS THEY WERE MEANT TO GROW

Energy Boosters versus Energy Drainers

Sometimes uncovering your hidden shadows is as easy as looking at how you feel in certain situations or with certain people. What makes you feel energized, alive or excited? And what makes you feel fatigued, bored or mentally exhausted?

List out what makes you feel energized and what drains you, both physically and emotionally. This can lead you to some exciting discoveries about how you could be spending your time, and what you should let go of.

My energy boosters are...

My energy drainers are...

The great courageous
act that we must all do,
is to have the courage to
step out of our history
and past so that we
can live our dreams.

OPRAH WINFREY

Affirmations for Acceptance

Shadow Work is about learning to love and accept yourself – your *whole* self – and affirmations can be helpful tools to remind us of our best qualities during our worst times. They have been found to stimulate more activity in certain areas of the brain and can help to increase objectivity and encourage behaviour change, so there are many reasons to use affirmations in daily life.

The most helpful affirmations are the ones that are completely personal to you, so use the next page to write five bespoke affirmations that will help you accept every layer of yourself. You can use some of the affirmations elsewhere in this book for inspiration, but try to make these specific to your situation so they resonate more.

It can also help to add these to places around your home so you see them regularly, such as on your bathroom mirror, on the fridge or inside your car's sun visor.

_____'s
Affirmations
for Acceptance

1. ....
....
....
....

2. ....
....
....
....

3. ....
....
....
....

4. ....
....
....
....

5. ....
....
....
....

*A good half
of the art of living
is resilience.*

ALAIN DE BOTTON

EVERY SINGLE
PART OF YOU
IS WORTHY OF
ACCEPTANCE.
EVERY.
SINGLE.
PART.

Healthy Boundaries

Shadow Work can be mentally and physically exhausting. You must create healthy boundaries in your life so you don't become overwhelmed by its emotional demands. Otherwise, you will lack the motivation to continue delving into Shadow Work as a long-term practice.

Use the space below to write down the three most stressful things in your life, and consider what boundaries you could put in place to ease the mental burden.

Here is an example: I feel overwhelmed when my partner doesn't help with chores, so I will tell them how I'm feeling and together we can divide tasks between ourselves so I have more time for my therapy appointments and journalling practice.

1.

....

....

2.

....

....

3.

....

....

Shadow Journal:
Perception

Journalling can be an incredibly helpful tool for Shadow Work, as sometimes writing down our feelings is easier than saying them out loud.

Use this lined page to explore the idea of perception by describing how you think other people see you and how that makes you feel. Remember, no one will ever read this, so you can be completely honest and open.

....

....

....

....

....

....

....

....

....

....

....

....

*I do not care
so much what I am
to others as I care
what I am to myself.*

MICHEL DE MONTAIGNE

DON'T WASTE
ANOTHER MINUTE
BEING ONLY HALF
OF YOURSELF.
THE REAL YOU IS
THE *WHOLE* YOU.

Manifest the Real You

Manifestation involves the law of attraction, which means turning your desires into reality through goal setting, visualization, intentional actions and taking proactive steps towards your desired future with clarity. The practice is used by many thought leaders the world over, and although it can seem a little far-fetched to some, the main aim is to get clear on what you want so you can be aware of and seize any relevant opportunities when they arise. However, without addressing your shadow self first, this will always stand in the way of you getting what you want most out of life.

You may want to start visualizing using this prompt:

Through Shadow Work, I am learning _____

about myself, which is making me feel less _____,

and more _____ .

Within the next _____ , I aim to _____

_____,

and I will do this by _____

_____.

When I picture myself a year from now, I am _____

_____

_____.

Vision Board

Now you have learned more about your shadow self and how it impacts your view of yourself, you can use this knowledge to think ahead to where you'd like to be a year from now. Use this page as a scrapbook to cut and stick any images or words that represent where you want to be in the next year.

Values

Shadow Work can lead us to all sorts of places and realizations, and one of those is understanding what we value most. If this isn't something you have thought about before, you can start to consider it as you work through this book and develop your Shadow Work further.

Circle which values are most relevant to your life and who you want to become. If you're stuck, you can look back at some of the other exercises in this book to discover what means the most to you.

Authenticity
Adventure
Balance
Community
Creativity
Fun
Friendship
Growth
Happiness
Honesty
Humour
Kindness
Love
Loyalty
Peace
Trust
Wisdom

Shadow Journal: Judgement

Use this page to explore the idea of judgement by writing about the last time you felt judgemental towards someone else. Where do you think those feelings came from? Do you feel this same judgement towards any of your own shadow traits? Be open and honest as you answer these questions.

By doing the work
to love ourselves more,
I believe we will love
each other better.

LAVERNE COX

LET GO OF JUDGING
AND BEING JUDGED.
WE ARE ALL JUST
TRYING TO DO OUR
BEST IN LIFE, SO
IT'S TIME TO HELP
EACH OTHER OUT.

*I like me.
I like my story and all
the bumps and bruises.
That's what makes
me uniquely me.*

MICHELLE OBAMA

Shadow Journal: Jealousy

Use this page to explore the idea of jealousy. Think about someone you feel jealous of. Why do you think you feel envious of them, rather than inspired by them? How does your jealousy impact your behaviour towards that person? How do you think this jealousy impacts your overall happiness and well-being? The person will never read this, so you can open up fully.

Integrating The Shadow in Action

Step one of Shadow Work is to identify the elements of our shadow self, and step two is about integrating the repressed parts of ourself with the version of us that exists on the outside. Repression can lead to feelings of resentment and a lack of fulfilment, but integrating our shadow self can help us to feel more whole, authentic and truthful.

The great thing about doing intentional Shadow Work is that, as each new realization comes to you, you get to decide which elements you integrate and which you reject.

Using the table on the next page, list some of the shadow characteristics you have learned about yourself from working through this book so far. Then, consider where each trait could be helpful or unhelpful. The first is an example, but you can add your own underneath.

SHADOW SELF	HELPFUL INTEGRATION	UNHELPFUL INTEGRATION
I feel a strong need to be perfect.	*I will integrate this trait at work as it could help me advance in my career.*	*I will reject this trait when it comes to my appearance as it often makes me feel sad and unworthy.*

LOOK TO OTHERS
AS INSPIRATION
AND MOTIVATION,
NEVER COMPETITION

How you love yourself
is how you teach
others to love you.

RUPI KAUR

YOU WILL NEVER REGRET SPENDING TIME AND ENERGY ON YOURSELF.

GIVE YOURSELF
THAT GIFT.

Shadow Journal: Peace

Use this page to explore the idea of peace by writing about what it means to you: Where were you and what were you doing the last time you truly felt at peace? How often would you like to have the feeling of peace? And what could you do to incorporate more peace into your life?

*Every breath we take,
every step we make,
can be filled with peace,
joy and serenity.*

THÍCH NHẤT HẠNH

Write a Letter to Your Inner Child

You will already have been thinking about your inner child (your deepest emotions and thoughts from childhood) throughout this book. Perhaps you have also been considering ways to talk to them and find out more about what they need and want. This is your chance to write a letter to your inner child using the space on the next page.

There are no rules here, just write about whatever comes up when you picture your inner child. If you need some idea for where to start, you could begin by writing down what has hurt you in the past, or by reassuring them you have their back. Remember to end your letter with some strategies to help your inner child feel better.

Dear Inner Child,

THE YOUNGER
VERSION OF YOU
WILL THANK YOU
ONE DAY FOR
DOING THE WORK,
AND SHINING LIGHT
ON THE SHADOWS

Insight Page

How are you feeling about your Shadow Work journey now? Write down any significant thoughts or feelings that have come up since you started working through this book, so you have something to look back on later when you continue your Shadow Work.

....

....

....

....

....

....

....

....

....

....

....

....

....

....

....

....

....

....

....

When your values
are clear to you,

*making decisions
becomes easier.*

ROY E. DISNEY

Pledge of Commitment

Shadow Work is an ongoing, lifelong process. If you are discouraged by the fact that your journey will never really be finalized, don't worry. The beauty of Shadow Work is how it never stops illuminating shadows, even when you think there's nothing left to work on.

You can continue to experience personal breakthroughs and revelations many years into the process, so it's a practice worth committing to. To make sure you don't start and stop Shadow Work, use the next page to write a declaration of your intent to carry on learning about yourself.

I, _____,

commit to casting light on my shadows, even when difficult
emotions come up. I will engage in daily or weekly

_____

to continue my personal growth, stay true to my values of

_____

_____

_____

and enjoy the lifelong process of getting to know myself better.

Signed,

_____

Seek Support

No one needs to go through Shadow Work alone, as it can bring up some complicated feelings and sad memories. Having support on your journey can really help keep you accountable to the practice and carry you through the tough days. This could be a registered therapist who can help with Shadow Work, or it could be a trusted family member or friend.

Write down three people who can be your support system throughout your Shadow Work journey, and how they may be able to help you on your way:

1.

....

....

....

2.

....

....

....

3.

....

....

....

SHADOW WORK
IS NEVER FINISHED.
STAY OPEN TO
CHANGE AND
KEEP GROWING.

Conclusion

Your shadow has many amazing qualities, and others that – although you might find them frustrating or saddening – can become some of your strongest attributes when integrated with your current self.

You have already built a fantastic foundation for Shadow Work that you can expand on for many years to come – congratulations! All the small exercises you have done will start you off on your Shadow Work journey. The practice can be difficult and confronting, but so worth it in the end.

Don't forget you can reach out for support from loved ones and/or a professional therapist as you tackle difficult memories or trauma – you never need to work through this alone.

As you continue to engage in Shadow Work, you can learn more and more about yourself, and show up to the world as the most authentic version of you. Good luck on your Shadow Work journey – everything you need to know is already inside of you, you just need to find it!

Resources

As well as the advice in this book, here are some additional sources that may provide further guidance on your Shadow Work journey.

Podcasts

Shadow Work Library
Hosted by Shadow Work educator Jessica Depatie, this podcast aims to help you illuminate your dark side so it can be an adventure rather than something to be feared, through exploring the root causes of negative patterning, shadow states and triggers.

The Inner Child Podcast
Hosted by coach and therapist Gloria Zhang, this weekly podcast aims to help those living with trauma to break free from toxic habits which may be a result of the trauma.

The Ego Project
Hosted by therapist Cristine Seidell and author Lisa Heidle, this podcast explores how a healthy or wounded ego impacts the relationship with the self and others, and how working on this can lead to healing.

Books

Julie Smith, *Why Has Nobody Told Me This Before?* (2022)

Bessel van der Kolk, *The Body Keeps the Score: Mind, Brain and Body in the Transformation of Trauma* (2015)

Nicole LePera, *How to Meet Your Self* (2022)

Brianna Wiest, *The Mountain Is You: Transforming Self-Sabotage Into Self-Mastery* (2020)

The Healing Workbook
Tips and Guided Exercises to Help Overcome Trauma

Amanda Marples | Paperback | ISBN: 978-1-80007-768-3

Begin your healing journey with this step-by-step workbook to help you understand and deal with trauma

The Healing Workbook contains practical advice, effective tips and guided exercises based on trusted cognitive behavioural therapy (CBT) techniques to help you begin the process of recovery. Within these pages you will find support and encouragement as you begin to come to terms with the past and find your way back to yourself, your values and a life where you can flourish and thrive.

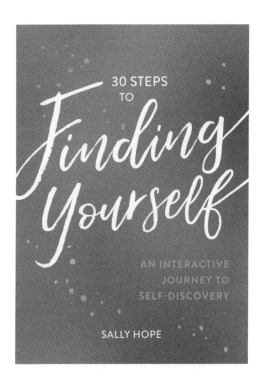

30 Steps to Finding Yourself
An Interactive Journey to Self-Discovery

Sally Hope | Paperback | ISBN: 978-1-83799-145-7

Build your self-esteem, grow your confidence and rediscover your sense of self with this empowering and practical 30-step journal for women

"Who am I?" The more confidently you are able to answer this question, the higher your levels of happiness, self-esteem and personal growth tend to be. However, in a world that still socializes women to build their lives around other people, many of us don't have an answer.

This 30-step journal will be your guide to understanding and empowering the most important person in your life: you.

Have you enjoyed this book?
If so, why not write a review on your favourite website?

If you're interested in finding out more about our books,
find us on Facebook at Summersdale Publishers,
on Twitter/X at @Summersdale and on Instagram
and TikTok at @summersdalebooks and get in touch.

We'd love to hear from you!

Thanks very much for buying this Summersdale book.

www.summersdale.com

IMAGE CREDITS